9/11/02

From:

Gary Cook

Christopher W.

Elvira Thurman

Wendy Cardone

Ronald Allan H. Amali

Justina Totouca

Denise S. Harrington

Moot Willson

Daniel D. Woodhouse

Rene B. Boongaling

A.J. Rabh

Jiewei R.

Jen Thurman

Slai Zoltan

Suminder Sidhu

Hyewon Kang

Amy Chery

Dennis S. Mayusha

Norma Khramornek

Ann Kathari

matthew Lew

Oleg Neustor

Laura Renteria

SAN FRANCISCO

A PICTORIAL SOUVENIR

CAROL M. HIGHSMITH AND TED LANDPHAIR

SAN FRANCISCO
A PICTORIAL SOUVENIR

CRESCENT BOOKS

NEW YORK

THE AUTHORS GRATEFULLY ACKNOWLEDGE THE SUPPORT PROVIDED BY

THRIFTY CAR RENTAL
SAN FRANCISCO
Jim and John Tennant, Owners

HOTEL DIVA

HOTEL GRIFFON

RENOIR HOTEL

IN CONNECTION WITH THE COMPLETION OF THIS BOOK

This 1999 edition is published by Crescent Books®,
an imprint of Random House Value Publishing, Inc.,
201 East 50th Street, New York, N.Y. 10022.

Crescent Books® and colophon are registered trademarks of
Random House Value Publishing, Inc.

Random House
New York • Toronto • London • Sydney • Auckland
http://www.randomhouse.com/

Printed and bound in China

*PAGES 2–3: The
Golden Gate Bridge
not only connects San
Francisco with the
Marin headlands and
the rest of Northern
California, it also
joins elements of the
spectacular Golden
Gate National
Recreation Area.*

Library of Congress Cataloging-in-Publication Data
Highsmith, Carol M., 1946–
San Francisco / Carol M. Highsmith and Ted Landphair.
p.   cm. — (A pictorial souvenir)
ISBN 0-517-20489-4 (hc: alk. paper)
1. San Francisco (Calif.)—Pictorial works. I. Landphair, Ted, 1942–   .
II. Title. III. Series: Highsmith, Carol M., 1946–   Pictorial souvenir.
F869.S343H53 1999   98–14197
979.4´61—dc21   CIP

8   7   6   5   4   3   2   1

Project Editor: Donna Lee Lurker
Designed by Robert L. Wiser, Archetype Press, Inc., Washington, D.C.

FOREWORD

San Francisco might well be the world's favorite city, such is the beauty of the natural and architectural sights, and the city's delightful eccentricities. It is more expensive to live here than anywhere else in America, but its citizens happily accept the high cost in return for its abundant charms: the freshest seafood, sourdough bread, and exotic international cuisines; world-class theater, art, ballet and opera; the lushest landscaped parks west of Philadelphia; and everyday vistas that prompt even lifelong San Franciscans to gasp in amazement. The city also seems to encourage people to "do his or her own thing" and is the home of some of the nation's most creative living arrangements—opposite and same-sex partnerships as well as roommate groupings of all descriptions.

Perfection? What about the earthquakes? The Great Quake of 1906 killed around one thousand people and destroyed much of the city, and the 1989 Loma Prieta quake flattened part of the San Francisco–Oakland Bay Bridge and sparked fires that consumed much of the Marina District. But only tourists ask such questions as natives are stoical on the subject: "What will be will be."

San Francisco is famed throughout the world for its cable cars and, of course, the Golden Gate Bridge—the No. 1 attraction among foreign visitors to the United States. But the heart of the city lies not with any individual attraction but the city's varied assortment of neighborhoods, each with its own distinct character. The Financial District is a medley of soaring skyscrapers that includes the great Transamerica Pyramid with its odd geometric supports—called "isosceles tetrahedrons." Not far away is Union Square, the city's chic shopping district, ringed by fine hotels and high-end stores. A few blocks away is Chinatown with its herbal pharmacies, curio shops, restaurants, and narrow alleys. Nearby is the one-mile-square Japantown ginza, a giant plaza surrounded by enchanting little gardens lined with bonsai trees.

North Beach is the home of kitschy theaters, jazz and comedy clubs, and Italian restaurants. At Fisherman's Wharf, the smells of fresh cooked crabs, hot sourdough bread, and chocolates from Ghirardelli Square swirl irresistibly. Ocean Beach lures surfers and hanggliders and nearby Golden Gate Park holds many attractions including the De Young art museum and the Japanese Tea Garden. The Panhandle, a tiny protruberence of the park, extends eastward into the Haight-Ashbury section, an eclectic neighborhood of Victorian houses and counterculturists. Above the Haight are some of the city's most prestigious neighborhoods including Pacific Heights, Inner and Outer Richmond, and Upper Fillmore. Close to downtown are elite Nob Hill and the less ritzy Tenderloin, the location of the city's soup kitchens and nudie shows.

Market Street, which plunges southwest from the Financial District and the Tenderloin past the Civic Center to the Castro neighborhood in Eureka Valley, is a familiar dividing line. The neighborhoods below Market, including "SoMa," are less expensive. Toward Mission Street is the city's Hispanic heartland—the Mission District—built around the 1791 Mission Dolores and now dotted with colorful grocery stores, flower shops, and exuberant murals.

In his rendition of the famous song about San Francisco, the great singer Tony Bennett left his heart there. It's little wonder, for the city is like a siren whose song once heard is never forgotten.

OVERLEAF: San Francisco's hills are not so noticeable at night when lights commingle into a galaxy-like display. Earthquake-resistant steel frame construction, with pilings sunk to bedrock, made high-rise construction possible.

Market Street (above), leading straight downtown, has been a dividing line between dense development to the north and less congestion to the south. Because of its affordability, developers of "SoMa," or South of Market, have been increasingly active here. The 1972 Transamerica Pyramid (opposite), San Francisco's tallest building, with its windowless "wings" —viewed here from an observation deck at the Mandarin Oriental Hotel—rises forty-eight stories, in addition to a 212-foot tower. Architect William Pereira chose the pyramidal configuration to bring more light to street level than a conventional skyscraper would have allowed. The tower is part of a block-long complex that includes lush Redwood Park and an outdoor performing stage. Embarcadero Center (overleaf) has been called a city within a city. This massive shopping, office, and hotel complex was built over fourteen years, beginning in 1967. Its four towers are linked by footbridges.

PAGES 12–13: Union Square is the heart of the city's shopping and hotel district. Winged Victory stands atop the square's monument, dedicated to Spanish-American War hero Admiral George Dewey in 1903.

The Wilderness Idea:

"It is hard to tell which has shaped the other more What does matter is that the mutuality was import

Ansel Adams and the
Sierra Club

PREVIOUS PAGES: *Yerba Buena Gardens built atop Moscone Convention Center facilities, offer a sparkling view of downtown, including the truncated cylindrical skylight of the San Francisco Museum of Modern Art. The Friends of Photography, a membership-supported arts organization, operates the Ansel Adams Center for Photography (above) in the Yerba Buena Gardens redevelopment area. It showcases the work of several photographers, including Adams, the pioneer wilderness photographer. He was heavily involved in the Sierra Club, and its image came to be defined by Adams's photographs. "I believe the approach of the artist and the approach of the environmentalist are fairly close," Adams once said, "in that both are, to a rather impressive degree, concerned with the 'affirmation of life.'" Dedicated in 1995, the San Francisco Museum of Modern Art (opposite), designed by Swiss architect Mario Botta in association with San Francisco's HOK firm, includes fifty thousand square feet of gallery space, almost doubling the exhibition space of its old Civic Center location. Its atrium opens onto studio spaces, a bookstore, and a café.*

More than 170 ferries once docked at the impressive Ferry Building (above) below Market Street. Built by state engineers beginning in 1895, the terminal was converted to office use after most ferries stopped running in the 1950s. The double-deck San Francisco–Oakland Bay Bridge (right), which opened in 1936, reaches the East Bay in two stages, meeting at Yerba Buena Island midway across the Bay. One upper end section of the bridge collapsed onto the lower level during the fearsome 1989 Loma Prieta earthquake. Amazingly, only one person died, and the bridge was reinforced and reopened in one month. Along the Embarcadero, the lampposts of Herb Caen Way (overleaf)—named for the late, beloved San Francisco Chronicle columnist—set a moody foreground for the bridge.

In the 1970s, Hollywood producer Francis Ford Coppola bought, remodeled, and established his American Zoetrope production studios in the flatiron Columbus Tower (opposite, foreground)—also called the Sentinel Building—in North Beach. It had just opened when the devastating 1906 earthquake struck and was one of the few downtown structures to survive. The corrupt Abe Ruef, an unelected power broker, once ran the city from this building. In North Beach, too, is the intimate Club Fugazi, home of Beach Blanket Babylon, the nation's longest-running musical revue—so long-running that an entire section of Green Street has been renamed "Beach Blanket Babylon Boulevard." Chanteuse Val Diamond (above) models one of the outrageously outsized hats for which the production is famous. The show is based loosely on Snow White's worldwide quest for her prince. Nearby Chinatown (overleaf) is one of the city's oldest and most densely populated neighborhoods.

The Bank of Canton is located in a building (opposite) that once housed a telephone exchange. Completed in 1909—three years after the Great Quake destroyed most of Chinatown—this pagoda was the first Chinese-style structure built in the city. Cantonese, rather than China's official Mandarin dialect, is the first language in much of Chinatown; the neighborhood's first residents were imported as mine and railroad workers from Canton and the surrounding province. Telephone exchange operators had to know five dialects and memorize the numbers of all of their customers. Callers would ask for their parties by name. Exotic shops and trading companies (left) still dot Chinatown, which has been reformed and modernized since the days when sinister gangs prowled and opium dens operated in the rear of several restaurants. Cable cars (overleaf) clatter up and down nearby Russian Hill every day.

Separate cables, whirring around giant wheels at a central power station (opposite), pull San Francisco's treasured cable cars along four routes, ranging in length from the 9,050-foot Powell Street line to 21,500 feet on California Street. The cables, made of steel wire wrapped around a natural-fiber core, must be replaced every 75 to 250 days. The cars, which travel at top speeds of 9.5 m.p.h., advance when their operators grab onto the moving cable with a grip that fits into a slot beneath the rails. The power station, at Washington and Mason streets, houses the city's free cable-car museum, where the story of the cars and the system's inventor, Andrew Smith Hallidie, is told. The most popular line with tourists ends at the foot of Hyde Street at a turnaround (above) reminiscent of those once functioning in railroad roundhouses.

The Hercules *tugboat (left) and the old ferry boat* Eureka *at the Hyde Street Pier (above) are exhibits at the San Francisco Maritime National Historic Park near Fisherman's Wharf. The* Hercules *originally hauled lumber, then hay stacked more than twenty feet high on its decks, up and down the Pacific Coast before switching to heavy-duty tugboat chores on San Francisco Bay. Before bridges crossed the Bay, the* Eureka *was one of the ferries that connected U.S. 101— the "Redwood Highway"—between San Francisco and Sausalito. Built in 1890, it began service as the railroad ferry* Ukiah. *Uphill from the maritime museum is Ghirardelli Square (overleaf)— pronounced "GEAR-ar-delly" — a shopping mecca in the 1900-vintage red-brick buildings of the old Ghirardelli chocolate factory.*

Dungeness crab— served inside and at a curbside steam table—and cioppino, a fish and shellfish dish cooked with tomatoes, wine, and spices, are specialties at Alioto's Restaurant (above), a Fisherman's Wharf institution run by one of San Francisco's most prominent families. Sea lions mysteriously appeared at Pier 39's west marina (right) shortly after the 1989 Loma Prieta earthquake.

Each winter, as many as six hundred vocifer- ous adult males— which can grow to 850 pounds—and adoles- cent animals of both sexes muscle for spots on the floating docks. Adult females stay close to breeding grounds as far away as Baja California, to which Pier 39's sea lions migrate each summer. Looking north from the pier, Alcatraz Island (overleaf) is a short ferry ride away.

Alcatraz. The word alone evokes stark images of desperate "cons" doing hard time in the bleak penitentiary in the middle of San Francisco Bay. From 1934 to 1963, Alcatraz Island was the home address to the "worst of the worst" federal prisoners, including Al Capone, George ("Machine Gun") Kelly, and Robert Stroud—the "Birdman of Alcatraz." Stroud actually never kept a canary on the island but earned his "Birdman" nickname previously at Leavenworth Penitentiary. In 1948, Frank Heaney (opposite), at age twenty-one, became the youngest man ever to serve on "The Rock." A born storyteller, Heaney—shown in the cellblock that the inmates wishfully called "Broadway"—later worked for the Blue & Gold ferry fleet, which carries more than a million visitors a year to the island. The burned-out warden's home (above) had earlier been an officers' club when Alcatraz was a military prison.

The Octagon House (opposite) stands next to a shady community park in San Francisco's Cow Hollow neighborhood—named for the dairy farms once located there that supplied most of the city's milk and cheese. Now a museum operated by the National Society of Colonial Dames, it displays decorative arts from the nation's Colonial and Federal periods. The house, with its illuminated cupola, was built in 1861 by William McElroy. It was one of eight octagonal homes built in town at a time when it was believed that eight-sided houses provided maximum light and ventilation. Affluent Pacific Heights boasts grand homes such as this mansion (top left) with its marvelous topiary landscaping. Many homes there and in Presidio Heights feature lovingly created Art Deco details (lower left).

The main campus of the University of San Francisco (above)— the city's oldest university—is located on a hill called "Lone Mountain" between Haight-Ashbury and Presidio Heights.

The Jesuit institution was founded in 1855, just six years after the great Gold Rush turned San Francisco from the sleepy Yerba Buena settlement into a boomtown that quickly became the

Queen City of the West. The 1914 Saint Ignatius Church serves the university and the surrounding community. In addition to its spectacular dome and campanile, it contains one of the city's most

beautiful sanctuaries (opposite). Its twin 210-foot towers are visible for miles, especially when they are lit at night. Because of its strong Asian, Hispanic, and even Russian influences, San Fran-

cisco boasts some of the nation's most diverse places of worship. Available are customized tours of Christian cathedrals, Jewish synagogues, and Chinatown temples.

PREVIOUS PAGES: One of San Francisco's most familiar postcard views—capturing both nearby Victorian houses and the distant downtown skyline—is taken from Alamo Square at Fulton and Steiner streets. It lies in the heart of a historic district that contains many of the city's fourteen thousand "painted ladies" as the houses are affectionately called. Ornamental pieces of many Queen Anne-style homes, including an 1890s house on Broderick Street (opposite), were ordered from catalogues. The Haas-Lilienthal House (left) in Pacific Heights is the only fully furnished San Francisco Victorian open to public tours. The Westerfield House (above) on Alamo Square was designed in 1889 by Henry Geilfuss in the "Stick" style made popular in Philadelphia. What appear to be visible support beams are purely decorative. More than fourteen thousand Victorian homes, of several styles, have been identified in San Francisco. Most are located west of Van Ness Avenue, where homes were dynamited to stop the spread of fires following the deadly 1906 earthquake.

It's been several decades since cries of "tune in, turn on, drop out" echoed throughout the "summer of love" in the hippie scene of San Francisco's Haight-Ashbury District. But "flower power" is well remembered in several shops along Haight Street. Positively Haight Street (above) is a colorful bead shop; Wasteland (opposite) sells vintage clothing and eclectic party supplies. "The Haight" is still home to eccentric coffee shops, cafés, and "head shops" selling marijuana paraphernalia. And young people with multicolored coiffures and ring-pierced noses, lips, and tongues still shuffle along the street. It's an almost nostalgic scene that's not lost on tour-bus operators who drive visitors out Haight Street regularly. But the neighborhood is carefully watched by police and has been largely gentrified. Detached "painted ladies" and elegant row houses in the Haight are now among the city's most desirable abodes.

The ornate Castro
Theater (above)—
built in 1923 as the
flagship movie palace
of the Nasser family
chain—is a landmark
in the Castro, the
world's largest openly
gay and lesbian neigh-
borhood. Once a
working-class Irish
community, the
Castro is famous for
its impromptu cele-
brations, especially on
Halloween. Its leaders
wield considerable
political clout at City
Hall. A fixture is the
Names Project store-
front, where volun-
teers continue to sew
sections of the giant
quilt that memorial-
izes AIDS victims.
Refurbished F-line
trolleys (right),
obtained from
Philadelphia and
painted to salute
seventeen cities where
the streetcars once
operated, run out of
Market Street. Golden
Gate Park's favorite
attraction is the
Japanese Tea Garden
(overleaf), built for
the Midwinter Fair
of 1894.

The Cliff House (left), is the third in a series of gathering places overlooking Seal Rocks at Ocean Beach. The second, spanning the turn of the twentieth century, was a Victorian palace that attracted visitors in droves. The current Cliff House also offers food, libations, and an extensive gift shop. Downstairs is the Musée Méchanique, an enchanting collection of coin-operated mechanical marvels from old penny arcades. Included are player pianos, strength-testing machines, and animated characters like the fortune teller (above). All work. Admission is free, but the temptation to spend a few quarters playing the contraptions is irresistible.

Commissioned officers and their families, stationed at the Presidio U.S. Army base, lived in modest quarters on Officers' Row (left). Each little home had a privy, garden, and chicken coop. The homes were not electrified until 1912. The Presidio fortification dates to 1776, when a Spanish captain claimed the land for his country. Mexican troops took control but were ousted by Americans during the "Bear Flag Revolt" of 1846. Thereafter, the Presidio gained a reputation as the "country club" of military posts. On the grounds, about fifteen thousand American soldiers lie in the military cemetery, whose vistas are reminiscent of Arlington National Cemetery outside Washington. There's even a whimsical pet cemetery (above) nearby. Closed by Congress in 1994, the Presidio is now a sprawling National Park Service site.

Fort Point (opposite and above) hunkers beneath the southern anchorage of the Golden Gate Bridge, where an extra steel arch was added to protect the fort below. A fortification has guarded the Golden Gate since 1794, when the Spanish, using Native American labor, completed an adobe fort known as El Castillo de San Joaquin. *Mexico gained control after its independence but abandoned El Castillo in 1835. U.S. Army engineers placed a ten-gun battery on the bluff above in 1855 as Fort Point was being constructed from more than eight million bricks and granite from California and China. The fort served as nerve center for construction of the Golden Gate Bridge (overleaf) between 1933 and 1937. Abandoned again, the fort was restored in the 1970s as a National Park Service site with extraordinary views of gun emplacements and the underbelly of the great bridge.*

Titles available in the Pictorial Souvenir series